WITHDRAWAL

AVAILABLE NOW
from Lerner Publishing Services!

The *On the Hardwood* series:

Boston Celtics
Brooklyn Nets
Chicago Bulls
Dallas Mavericks
Houston Rockets
Indiana Pacers
Los Angeles Clippers
Los Angeles Lakers

Miami Heat
Minnesota Timberwolves
New York Knicks
Oklahoma City Thunder
Philadelphia 76ers
Portland Trail Blazers
San Antonio Spurs
Utah Jazz

COMING SOON!

Additional titles in
the *On the Hardwood* series:

Atlanta Hawks
Cleveland Cavaliers
Denver Nuggets
Detroit Pistons
Golden State Warriors
Memphis Grizzlies
Phoenix Suns
Washington Wizards

To Order • www.lernerbooks.com • 800-328-4929 • fax 800-332-1132

ON THE HARDWOOD

ZACH WYNER

1967 World Champions

Perhaps sports are never more important than when the world we live in is changing. Change is never easy. When difficult times are upon us, and it's hard to make sense of the enormous, complicated world outside our front door, sports soothe our anxieties and fears. But sports are more than just a distraction; they are a source of optimism and hope. Athletes that work together, challenge one another, sacrifice for one another, and compete as a team, inspire us. They instill in us the belief that anything is possible.

1967 was a tumultuous time. The United States was involved in a war in Vietnam, a small country in Southeast Asia. By April of that year, many important historical figures, including boxing legend

The Times They Are A-Changin'

The Civil Rights Movement and the Anti-War Movement were at the center of the American experience in 1967.

Muhammed Ali and civil rights leader Dr. Martin Luther King, Jr., had publicly criticized the war. Huge demonstrations took place across the country with thousands of Americans assembling to show the government that they wanted peace instead of war. In addition to anti-war demonstrations, the Civil Rights Movement was in full swing. African-Americans were demanding to be treated the same as everyone else. In Philadelphia, a city with a large African-American population, black students asked public schools to include the African-American perspective in their history classes. When the schools refused, those students walked out in protest.

In this turbulent time, the historic city of Philadelphia needed a symbol of unity and hope. In April of 1967, they found that symbol in a basketball team.

For four years the Philadelphia 76ers had been competitive. In fact, before moving to Philadelphia in 1963, they had even won an NBA championship as the Syracuse Nationals in 1955. However, since the move, they had managed only to be second best to Bill Russell and the dominant Boston Celtics. From 1958 to 1966 the Boston Celtics won an astounding eight straight NBA championships. During this span, they had knocked the Nationals/76ers out of the playoffs five straight times—including twice since their move to Philly in 1963. However, as the 1966-67 season got underway, it began to look as though no team could stand between

Wilt Chamberlain and Bill Russell gather for the opening tip-off of the 1967 Eastern Conference Finals.

Philadelphia and the ultimate prize.

Led by the legendary center Wilt "The Stilt" Chamberlain (who once scored 100 points in a single game against the New York Knicks), the Sixers charged out of the gate. They steamrolled the rest of the league on their way to a 46-4 record. As dominant as Chamberlain was, winning 46 out of 50 games was not something he could have done by himself. Philadelphia's other stars, players like Chet Walker, Lucious Jackson, Wali Jones, and Hall of Famers Hal Greer and Billy Cunningham, were all key contributors. While those names may not be familiar to you, at the time they were some of the best players in the world. With Wilt "The Stilt" towering over the competition,

Chet Walker attempts an acrobatic shot over Sam Jones.

9

there was little the rest of the league could do to stop the Sixers.

Wilt Chamberlain is considered by many to be the most dominant center ever to play the game of basketball. Born and raised in Philadelphia, Wilt was a homegrown star. In high school, he was a giant among boys, leading his Overbrook Panthers to back-to-back city championships. He entered the pros in 1959, and at 7'1" and 275 pounds, he was eight inches taller and 67 pounds heavier than the average NBA player. Wilt made good use of that size. In 1962, he averaged over 50 points and 25 rebounds per game! However, under 76ers coach Alex Hannum, Wilt agreed to get his teammates involved in the offense. He had won the NBA's Most Valuable Player award twice; what he wanted now was a championship. After watching the Celtics win year after year, Wilt realized that great teams would always triumph over a great player. He was going to do everything in his power to make the 1967 Sixers a great team.

Even with the 76ers dominating the regular season, and finishing with an amazing win/loss record of 68-13 (the best in league history at that point in time), some doubted whether they could actually dethrone the World Champion Boston Celtics. These doubters had good reason to be skeptical. Under player/coach Bill Russell, the Celtics had not exactly taken the year off. They had finished second in the Eastern Conference with a record of

60-21. The stage was set for an epic battle, one that would be discussed for many years to come.

For years, Wilt Chamberlain had been regarded as a loner. Playing for the Philadelphia Warriors, a team that lacked a consistent second scoring option, he averaged 50.4 points per game in 1962. But critics were quick to point out that Wilt's prolific scoring never resulted in an NBA title. In Game 1 of the Eastern Conference Finals, Wilt silenced those critics by showing them what he was capable of when surrounded by great players.

A triple double (when a player achieves double digits in at least three statistical categories such as points, rebounds, assists, blocks or steals) is a special achievement. In the history of the NBA, only three players (Jason Kidd, Magic Johnson, and Larry Bird) have had more than ten

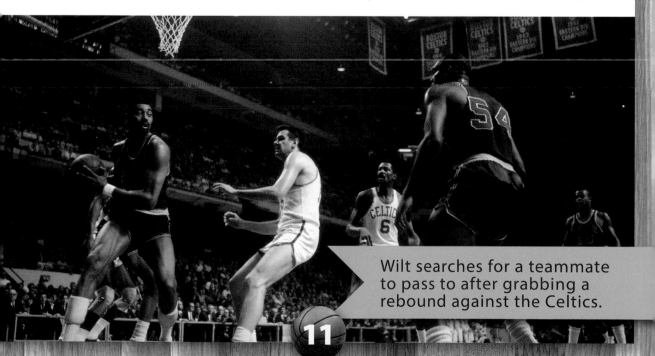

Wilt searches for a teammate to pass to after grabbing a rebound against the Celtics.

playoff triple-doubles. In Game 1 of the 1967 Eastern Conference Finals, Wilt Chamberlain did something that none of those great players ever did—he had a Quadruple Double!

Chamberlain soars for a rebound over 11-time NBA champion Bill Russell.

Wilt scored 24 points, grabbed 32 rebounds, dished out 13 assists, and recorded 12 blocks! While his 13 assists demonstrated his unselfishness, the 14-point victory by the 76ers showed what a group of stars was capable of when they trusted one another and played together as a team.

If the ever-prideful Celtics believed that things would return to normal after that game, they were wrong. This 76ers team was different from the ones in the past. The teamwork they demonstrated in Game 1 was no fluke. They had been doing this all season. And neither Wilt nor his teammates were satisfied with one historic game. The Sixers continued to dominate play, taking a 3-1 series lead. Then, in the final game of the series, ecstatic Sixers fans roared their approval, as the 76ers scored 140 points. Walker, Greer, Jones, Cunningham, and Chamberlain each scored over 20 points. The team that had set the record for the most wins in the regular season had finally done what no other team had done for nearly a decade: beat Boston.

After slaying the mighty Celtics, the 76ers faced a formidable challenge in the talented San Francisco Warriors. Rick Barry was the Warriors star forward and NBA scoring leader at 35 points per game. They also had a talented young center, Nate Thurmond, who had learned much under the tutelage of Wilt when Wilt had played for the Warriors. The Western Conference Champion could not be taken lightly. But the Sixers had not come this far only to fail. They beat the Warriors in six games. The 76ers had their first NBA title, and a divided city had a common cause to celebrate. To this day, basketball experts consider the 1966-67 Philadelphia 76ers to be one of the greatest teams ever assembled.

Al Attles drives an open lane for a lay-up while Wilt battles for rebounding position.

Chapter 2

DOCTOR'S ORDERS

In the year that followed their 1967 championship, the Sixers again dominated league play. Many believed they were on their way to being the next great basketball dynasty. However, after opening up a 3-1 series lead against the Celtics in the 1968 Eastern Conference Finals, the Sixers fell flat. They lost the next three games and finished the season in defeat. The Celtics went on to win yet another championship; the 76ers, desperate to regain the upper hand over Boston, went on to make one of the most controversial trades in NBA history.

Basketball is about more than what you see on the court. Coaching and

personnel decisions factor just as heavily into a team's fortunes as defense, rebounding, or a well-executed pick and roll. After losing

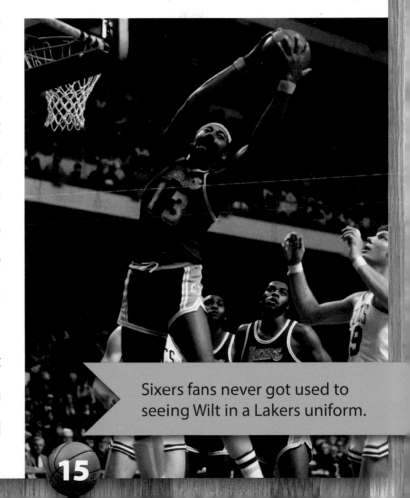

Sixers fans never got used to seeing Wilt in a Lakers uniform.

to the Celtics in the 1968 playoffs, the Sixers felt they needed to do something bold in order to make it back to the NBA Finals. In addition to this, their star player, Wilt Chamberlain, was requesting a trade. Unable to resolve their differences, management dealt Wilt to the Los Angeles Lakers. Unfortunately for the Sixers, the move did not pay off. For the next three seasons, the team never made it past the second round of the playoffs. Then, in the 1972-73 season, the bottom fell out. The Sixers won only nine games and lost 73. Nothing drains the joy from basketball like a losing season. Fortunately for the Sixers and their fans, a doctor was on the way.

Basketball is constantly evolving – rules, strategies, styles of play and the length of the players' shorts all change. Never was change more visible, more sudden or more thrilling then when a man called Julius "Dr. J" Erving came to Philadelphia. Everything about Dr. J—from his giant Afro to his jaw-dropping

Wilt grabs a rebound against his former team.

dunks—looked different from his predecessors. But it looked different in a way that awed and inspired countless young fans. The Doctor was brought to Philadelphia to heal an ailing 76ers team, but he did more than just that. He forever altered the way the game was played.

By 1976, Dr. J had been playing professional basketball (and had been winning professional basketball championships) for years. He just hadn't been doing it in the NBA. Dr. J's championships were won in the American Basketball Association (ABA), a professional basketball league formed in the 1960s. For a while, the ABA was considered inferior to the NBA. However, after a few years of exhibition games (in which the ABA

Dr. J led the New York Nets to the 1976 ABA Championship against the Denver Nuggets.

players proved to be every bit as good as the NBA players), the two leagues merged. The Indiana Pacers, San Antonio Spurs, Denver Nuggets, and Dr. J's ABA Champion New York Nets joined the NBA. Luckily for

Monster Numbers
During his 1975-76 MVP season, Dr. J averaged 29 points, 11 rebounds, five assists, three steals, and two blocks per game.

Hallowed Ground

Numerous other stars, including Kareem Abdul-Jabbar, Earl "The Pearl" Monroe, and Wilt Chamberlain, also played at Rucker Park before becoming NBA stars.

76ers fans, the New York Nets could no longer afford their best player. Just two days before the 1976-77 season was set to begin, Dr. J was traded to the 76ers.

Dr. J soars 15 feet through the air, en route to winning the 1976 ABA Slam Dunk title.

Julius Erving was the ABA's biggest star. Raised in Roosevelt, New York, he had earned the nickname "Dr. J" while playing pick-up games at legendary Rucker Park in Harlem. Opposing players called him "Doctor" because of his ability to carve up defenses like a surgeon. As a pro, he brought the flair of street ball to the NBA. Dr. J dazzled fans with his above-the-rim acrobatics, and in 1976, he won the first ever slam-dunk contest. His signature dunk, one that only a few players (including Michael Jordan and Vince Carter) have been able to duplicate, was the free-throw line dunk. Dr. J would stand on the far end of the court, 94 feet from the basket, and take off at a jog. As he crossed mid-court, his speed increased, his strides long and graceful like a gazelle. Then, just before reaching the free-throw line, he took flight. Time stood still as he lifted through the air, the ball held high over his head. He descended on the basket swiftly, bringing the ball down like a sledgehammer and slamming it through the hoop.

With the addition of Dr. J, the 1976-77 Sixers had much in common with the 2008 Boston Celtics and the 2011 Miami Heat. Like the Celtics of 2008 with Kevin Garnett, Paul Pierce, and Ray Allen, and the Heat of 2011 with LeBron James, Dwyane Wade, and Chris Bosh, people wondered if a team of All-Stars could share the spotlight and play together.

The Sixers had a strong inside presence in George McGinnis, a

McGinnis was a star for the ABA's Indiana Pacers before being traded to the 76ers.

muscular 6'8", 235-pound power forward. Shooting guard World B. Free lit things up from the outside and used his 44-inch vertical leap to soar over opponents. Sharp-shooting future coach Doug Collins scored nearly 20 points per game. By adding Dr. J to the mix, the 76ers suddenly had one of the most dynamic and exciting teams in the league. The question was: would these stars be willing to sacrifice some of their individual statistics for the good of the team? That question was answered when the 76ers finished the season in first place.

The 1976-77 playoffs were hard fought. On their way to the NBA Finals, the Sixers defeated the rival Celtics as well as the Moses Malone-led Houston Rockets. Having beaten these teams, the Sixers then took the first two games of the NBA Finals from Bill Walton's Portland Trail Blazers. They were confident that the trophy was theirs. It seemed as though

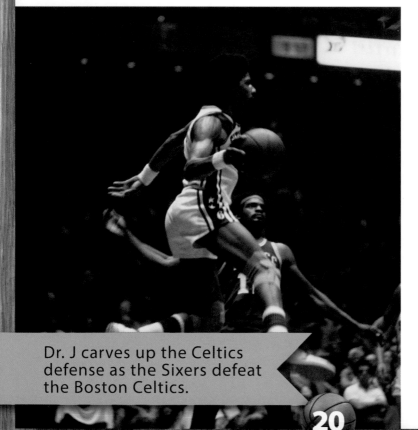

Dr. J carves up the Celtics defense as the Sixers defeat the Boston Celtics.

no team had the answer to the question: how do you stop a team of All-Stars? Sadly, the answer wasn't as complicated as many thought. Ball movement, team defense, and the great play of Trail Blazers center, Bill Walton, were the tools Portland used to storm back. After trailing 0-2, Portland won the series 4-2.

Bitterly disappointed by the way their season had ended, the 76ers would return the next season with the motto: "We owe you one." However, while they had fallen short of their goal, no one could overlook what they had achieved. Just four years after setting the NBA record for fewest wins, the 76ers had come within two games of winning a championship. They had restored their image as one of the league's

On a Roll
Before beating the Sixers 4-2, Bill Walton and the Trail Blazers swept Kareem Abdul-Jabbar and his Lakers, 4-0.

fiercest and best teams, and they had regained the respect of their fans. While the 1976-77 Sixers failed to bring a basketball championship back to Philly, they succeeded in bringing Philly back to basketball.

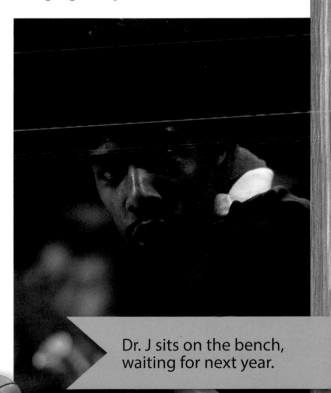

Dr. J sits on the bench, waiting for next year.

Chapter 3
BIG MO AND SIR CHARLES

During the next five seasons, the 76ers were a team that no one wanted to face. Everyone in the league knew that, on a given night, the Sixers had the talent to crush any opponent. But while their talent meant winning seasons and playoff appearances, it did not mean championships. The Sixers had come oh-so close in 1977. They again made the NBA Finals in 1980 and 1982. Each time they fell. You see, in 1979 a pair of superstars, going by the names Magic Johnson and Larry Bird had exploded onto the scene. Now their two teams (the Los Angeles Lakers and the Boston Celtics) seemed poised to rule the NBA for years to come. In 1980 and 1982, Dr. J and the Sixers fell to Magic Johnson's Lakers in the NBA

Finals. In 1981, it was Larry Bird's Celtics that defeated them in the East. The hope spawned by the 1977 team seemed a distant memory, and Sixers fans feared that their team would never be good enough to beat both Boston and L.A. Those fears were put to rest when a man named Moses came to town.

Moses Malone, also known as "Big Mo" or "Chairman of the Boards" (as he was called for his incredible rebounding skills) was one of the first players to jump straight from high school to professional basketball. As a senior at Petersburg High in Virginia, Moses had been recognized

Moses Malone gets fed the ball in the low post against the Washington Bullets.

more physical. While many thought his move straight to the pros was a mistake, no one could argue with the results. By the time Big Mo joined the 76ers, he was already a two-time MVP. He had led the Houston Rockets to the NBA Finals in 1981, averaged over 31 points per game in 1981-82 and twice set the record for most offensive rebounds in a season. At 6'10" and 235 pounds, he was the most dominant frontcourt presence to wear a 76ers uniform since Wilt "The Stilt" Chamberlain.

The 1982-83 Sixers were not a two-man show. Playing alongside Moses and Dr. J were All-Stars Maurice Cheeks, Andrew Toney, and Bobby Jones. In fact, in 1983, the Sixers had a league-high 4 All-Stars, with Cheeks, Malone, and Erving all

as the top high school talent in the land. He had been recruited by nearly 300 universities! But Mo had examined the college game and decided he wanted something

Prince of Soul
Sung at the 1983 NBA All-Star Game, Marvin Gaye's version of "The Star-Spangled Banner" is remembered as one of the greatest versions of the song ever performed.

in the starting line-up for the East. 76ers team defense was stout, and with Dr. J, Moses, and Andrew Toney all averaging over 20 points per game, this Sixers team could flat-out score the basketball.

The 1982-83 Sixers won 65 games. When asked how he thought his team would fare in the playoffs, Big Mo uttered the famous prediction "fo, fo, fo," (meaning the Sixers would sweep each playoff series in four games and win the championship). While the team fell just short of his prediction, losing one playoff game to the Milwaukee Bucks, they did win their second NBA title

since moving to Philadelphia. That season, Big Mo won both the regular season MVP as well as the NBA Finals MVP, and he saved his best for last. In Game 4 of the NBA Finals, Moses completely outplayed Los Angeles Lakers Hall of Fame center Kareem

Moses looks to pass out of the double-team set by Kareem Abdul-Jabbar and Kurt Rambis.

Moses prepares to take the Larry O'Brien trophy for a spin in the 76ers Championship parade.

Abdul Jabbar, scoring 24 points and grabbing 24 rebounds!

In 1982, the 76ers had fallen in the NBA Finals to the Los Angeles Lakers 4-2. In 1983, they swept the Lakers 4-0. Thanks to the presence of Big Mo, Dr. J was able to win his first and only NBA title. Thanks to great coaching and one of the league's all-time best starting fives, Philly fans were treated to a season regarded by NBA.com as one of the 10 greatest of all time.

The three seasons that followed the 1983-84 Sixers were disappointing. Dr. J, while still productive, could no longer be relied on to score over 20 points, grab seven to eight rebounds and guard the other team's best player for 40 minutes every night. Big Mo's production stayed about the same, but by the end of the 1985-86 season, management determined that things needed to change. They traded Moses Malone to the Washington Bullets and began to build around their budding superstar, Charles Barkley.

Only four players in the history of the NBA compiled over 20,000 points, 10,000 rebounds and 4,000 assists: Wilt Chamberlain, Kareem Abdul Jabbar, Karl Malone, and Charles Barkley. The numbers were just about the only thing Charles had in common with these other players. Chamberlain and Jabbar were both seven-foot centers that used height, power, and grace to command the post. At 6'9" and 250 muscular pounds, Karl Malone was perhaps the strongest power forward in the history of the league. Listed at 6'6", Barkley was actually closer to 6'4". Still, he controlled the boards and created shots for himself and his teammates like few forwards before or since. His outstanding play made him part of basketball royalty and earned him the nickname "Sir Charles."

Born in Leeds, Alabama, Barkley was one of those rare NBA talents who did not receive much attention during high school. He struggled with his weight, and did not even make the varsity team until his senior year—when a late growth spurt pushed him form 5'10" to 6'4". Although Charles put up excellent numbers that season, it wasn't until

Loaded Draft
Barkley was one of three Hall of Famers selected in the top five in the 1984 NBA Draft. The other two were Hakeem Olajuwon and Michael Jordan.

the state semifinals that college recruiters noticed him. During the Alabama state tournament, an assistant coach from the University of Auburn reported seeing "a fat guy… who can play like the wind." In 2006, that "fat guy" would be inducted into the NBA Hall of Fame.

Sir Charles has been called many things by the media including "outspoken," "controversial," and "outrageous." However, the word that defined him best as a player was "relentless." Fans of Sir Charles remember him best for snatching a defensive rebound, driving the length of the court and soaring over defenders for a fearsome dunk.

Besides being remembered as the premiere player for Philadelphia, Sir Charles is also remembered for being the leading scorer on the first USA Olympic Dream Team. On a team that included Michael Jordan, Larry Bird and Magic Johnson, it was Sir Charles who led the team with 18 points per game while shooting 71% from the field!

At his worst, Charles was a ballplayer whose emotions and desire to win caused him to make some embarrassing mistakes. At his best, Charles was a man who took responsibility for his mistakes and spoke the truth as he saw it. He initiated meaningful discussions about basketball players and whether or not they should be thought of as role models. While his opinions have ignited controversy, his intelligence, wit, and outspoken nature make him a household name to this day. As an analyst, Barkley appears on TNT multiple nights a week to comment on the play of today's basketball stars.

Charles may never have won a championship, but that doesn't diminish what he accomplished as a player. He transformed himself from a chubby kid with a knack for rebounding, into one of the game's all-time greats. As a member of the 76ers, Charles led the team in scoring and rebounding for six straight years. He was also at his best when it mattered most. From the 1985-86 season through his final season with the Sixers in 1991, Sir Charles averaged 25 points and 12 rebounds during the playoffs. Barkley never brought an NBA title to Philadelphia, but everyone who watched him play knew that it wasn't for lack of effort. Sir Charles left it all on the court.

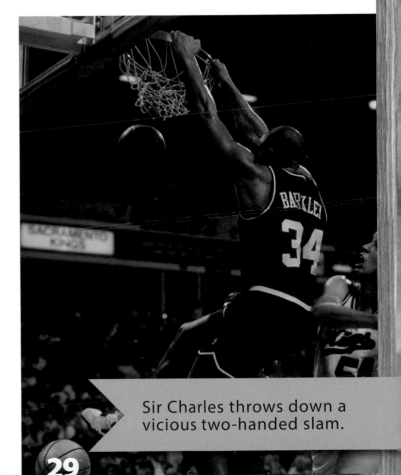

Sir Charles throws down a vicious two-handed slam.

Chapter 4
EVERY QUESTION HAS AN ANSWER

After missing the playoffs in 1992, Barkley wanted out of Philly. The Sixers had been on the decline and he wanted to play for a contender. When other teams know that a player is unhappy, it is very difficult to get a player of equal talent to the one you're trying to trade. The trade that moved Charles Barkley not only hurt the 76ers, it angered fans. In this respect, it was eerily reminiscent of the dark days that followed the departure of Wilt Chamberlain. Charles went to the Phoenix Suns where he promptly won the league MVP and led the Suns to the NBA Finals. The 76ers struggled for the next four seasons, hitting a low point in 1996 when they finished the regular season with a record of 18-64. The question

Adding Insult to Injury
In his first season in Phoenix, Barkley averaged 26 points, 12 rebounds, five assists, and led the Suns to a 62-20 record.

on the minds of 76ers fans was: how in the world are we going to become competitive again? Happily for them, an answer was on the way.

Charles Barkley poses for a photo with his 1993 NBA MVP trophy.

By the time he entered college, Allen Iverson was already a controversial figure. Born into absolute poverty, Iverson had overcome all odds to become a star high school basketball and football player. He had national attention and seemed destined for sports stardom. Then on February 14th, 1993, everything changed. That night at a bowling alley in Virginia, what began as a shouting match between two groups of teenagers, erupted into a brawl. Iverson was arrested and sentenced to 15 years in prison for his role in the fight. His sentence was eventually overturned for lack of evidence, but not before Iverson had spent four months in jail. Iverson was released, but many universities no longer wanted him. Coach John Thompson at Georgetown University looked past the criminal record. He

Iverson leads the Georgetown Hoyas to victory.

believed that Iverson could be a great player and a good citizen. He would be rewarded for his belief in this young athlete's character. In his two years at Georgetown, Iverson won two Big East Defensive Player of the Year awards, the Big East Rookie of the Year, and became Georgetown's all-time leader in career scoring average with 23 points per game.

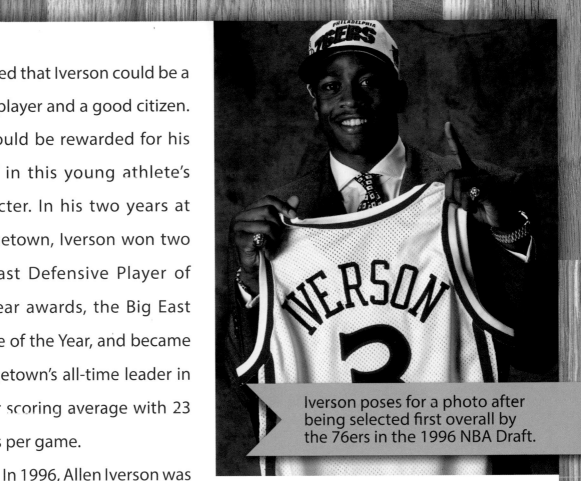

Iverson poses for a photo after being selected first overall by the 76ers in the 1996 NBA Draft.

In 1996, Allen Iverson was selected with the first pick in the NBA draft by the Philadelphia 76ers. The team had found an answer to their problems and the city had found a star. Unlike Philly stars before him, Iverson would not dominate with his size. He would not soar from the free-throw line for any dunks. He would not patrol the paint and intimidate the offense with his height and shot-blocking ability. He would not set league records for rebounding. What he did was lead the league in steals, terrorizing offensive players with his quickness and instincts for the ball, and become the smallest

Iverson single-handedly carves up the New Jersey Nets' defense.

Answer" for a variety of reasons, Iverson was the answer to all the Sixers' problems.

Not everyone appreciated Iverson the way Sixers fans did. The media referred to him as a polarizing player—meaning that people either loved him or hated him. With cornrows in his hair and a variety of tattoos, Iverson looked less businesslike than other NBA players. While his appearance might have confused some people, those people were out of touch with the new culture of basketball.

Raised in poverty by a hard-working teenage mother, Iverson was the new face of basketball: a young man who had seen the

player ever to lead the league in scoring–a feat he accomplished four times. Standing six feet tall and weighing 160-pounds, Iverson used unbelievable quickness, court awareness and scoring ability to become the smallest player ever to win league MVP. Nicknamed "The

sport as a way to provide for his family. 76ers fans knew this about him and they loved him for it. And regardless of what others thought of him, no one could ignore his skills. Iverson's crossover dribble, a move that regularly caused defenders to literally fall over while trying to guard him, became one of the game's most unstoppable and

Tape Up Those Ankles
On March 12th, 1997, Allen Iverson crossed over nine-time all defensive first teamer Michael Jordan. This highlight continues to get millions of views on YouTube.

most imitated moves.

Basketball is a team game. It has been demonstrated time and again that the best team will always come out ahead. However, that does not mean that there isn't room for individual expression.

The Answer crosses over and blows by Andre Miller.

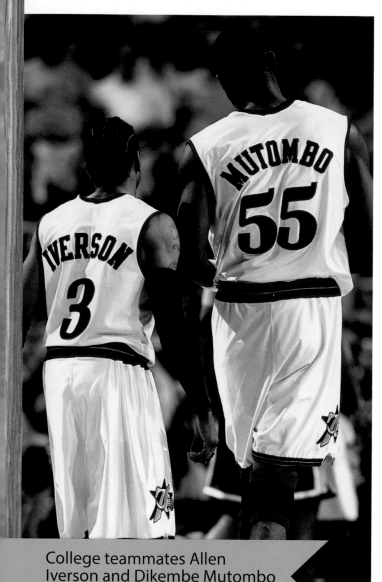

College teammates Allen Iverson and Dikembe Mutombo are reunited in Philly.

Iverson's ball-handling skills helped create the same thing as a series of screens and passes: an open shot. When he left defenders in the dust and drove to the basket, other defenders had to help. This created easy looks for his teammates.

In the 2000-01 season, no team demonstrated greater unity and character than Allen Iverson's 76ers. Coached by Larry Brown, a man considered one of basketball's great teachers, Iverson became a willing student.

With Allen Iverson as the centerpiece of the offense, Philadelphia improved their defense. They brought in Aaron McKie and George

Lynch, terrific defenders with a knack for getting steals. Then, after losing center Theo Ratliff to injury, the Sixers made a giant trade. They acquired Iverson's former teammate at Georgetown, 7'1" center Dikembe Mutombo. Mutombo would go on to block shots as though he were the reincarnation of Wilt Chamberlain and win the Defensive Player of the Year. He was not the only 76er to take home an award that season. Aaron McKie was named 6th Man of the Year, Larry Brown was Coach of the Year, and Iverson won the MVP.

The 76ers finished the season with the best record in the East, but they had to scratch and claw their way to the NBA Finals. Facing Reggie Miller's Indiana Pacers in the first round and Vince Carter's Toronto Raptors in round two, took its toll. Iverson's 160-pound body was beginning to break down. The countless hard fouls he'd taken on aggressive drives to the rim caused a significant dip in his shooting percentage. Needing a few days to heal, Iverson was forced to sit out Game 3 of the Eastern

Iverson and coach Larry Brown discuss strategy during the 2001 playoffs.

Iverson attempts a shot over Lakers' center Shaquille O'Neal.

Avoiding the Sweep

In the history of the NBA, no team has ever gone undefeated in a postseason.

Conference Finals against the Milwaukee Bucks. However, despite his nagging injuries, he came back to play some of the best games of his career when it mattered most.

With Iverson playing through pain, he recovered his shooting touch in Game 6 against the Bucks. He scored 26 of his 46 points in the fourth quarter. The Sixers lost that game, but the momentum they gathered in the fourth quarter carried over into Game 7. Iverson scored 44 and the Sixers won by 17.

2001 marked the Sixers' first trip to the NBA Finals since Moses and Dr. J had won it all in 1983. However, this time, no one expected the Sixers to win. The Los Angeles Lakers came into the 2001 NBA Finals winners of 11 straight playoff games. They were threatening to do exactly what Moses had predicted the Sixers would do in 1983: sweep their way to a championship.

The 2001 Sixers won Game 1 of the NBA Finals in Los Angeles in overtime, shocking the basketball world. Allen Iverson scored 48 points and snatched five steals, while Dikembe Mutombo grabbed 16 rebounds and swatted five blocks. It would be the last game they won that season. Still, while the Sixers were unable to stop Shaquille O' Neal, Kobe Bryant, and the Lakers, they never gave in. Taking their lead from Iverson, a star who played his heart out every night for his team and his family, the 2001 76ers made the city of Philadelphia proud.

76ers fans show pride in their team during a Game 5 loss to the Lakers.

Chapter 5
FOLLOW THE LEADER

Creating and maintaining a successful basketball team is a lot like managing a successful classroom. Players, just like students, need to be willing to work together. In addition to this, the teacher, no matter how smart and how talented, must earn the students' respect and trust. Without respect and trust, the class cannot succeed.

Following the 2001 season, the 76ers never quite managed to get their classroom in order. Then, after a disappointing second-round playoff loss to the Detroit Pistons in 2003, Larry Brown left Philadelphia. While Iverson and Brown had been struggling to get along, the move was still a bit of a surprise. The Sixers' Hall of Fame coach quit his job to become the head coach of the Detroit Pistons. To add insult to injury, Brown's Pistons went on to win the championship the very next year. Meanwhile, the Sixers would fall further out of contention. While Larry Brown's Pistons were beating the Los Angeles Lakers in the 2004 NBA Finals, the Sixers were at home, watching on TV. They had failed to make the playoffs for the first time

Eric Snow attempts to penetrate a clogged lane against the New Jersey Nets.

in six years.

In subsequent years, the 76ers tried a number of things (such as bringing in All-Star forward Chris Webber) to help revitalize the team. Things never quite worked out the way they'd hoped. Then, after a terrible start to the 2006-07 campaign, the Sixers and "The Answer" parted ways. Allen Iverson was traded to Denver. The 76ers talented swingman, Andre Iguodala, became the team's new leader.

Andre Iguodala (referred to as "Iggy" by his fans) led the Sixers to the playoffs four times, and in the 2012 playoffs, the 76ers won their first playoff series in ten years against the Chicago Bulls. The Bulls had lost star point guard Derrick Rose to a torn ACL, but this did not diminish the Sixers' achievement. In beating the Bulls, they became just the third #8 seed in the history

Andre Igoudala at the free throw line. In 2008 he averaged a career-high 20 points per game.

of the NBA to beat a #1 seed. From there, the games only got bigger. Two weeks after their historic achievement, the 76ers proved to the rest of the league that their victory against the Bulls was no fluke.

In the second round of the 2012 playoffs, the 76ers found themselves pitted against a familiar opponent: the Boston Celtics. Many experts thought this series would be a Celtics sweep. However, trailing in the series three games to two, the 2012-13 76ers showed what they were capable of.

Game 6 was just what the Sixers wanted: a defensive struggle. Still, every time they pulled ahead, the Celtics countered. With Sixers fans growing fearful that the season

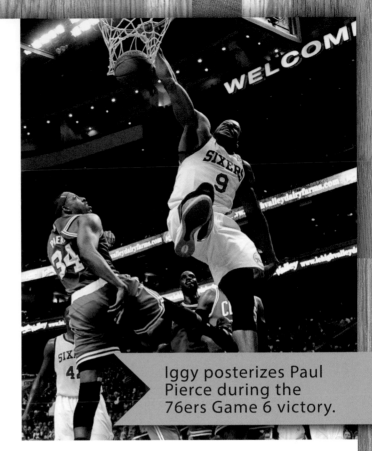

Iggy posterizes Paul Pierce during the 76ers Game 6 victory.

might end before their eyes, Iggy struck. His vicious dunk over Paul Pierce sent the fans into a frenzy. Then, with just over a minute left in the quarter and the Sixers clinging to a three-point lead, Iggy knocked down a deep three. The 76ers wouldn't need much more scoring that night to seal the victory. Doug

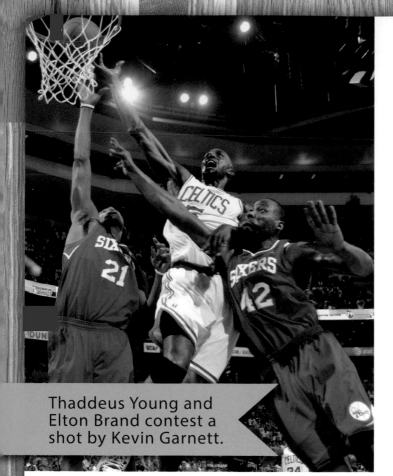

Thaddeus Young and Elton Brand contest a shot by Kevin Garnett.

fought Game 7 in Boston, their youthful players gained something invaluable: playoff experience. Five of their best players were under the age of 24, but this group knew what it was like to play when the lights were shining brightest and the entire basketball world was watching. Sixers fans had reason to be hopeful. Still, many of them stopped short of hoping that a single offseason would be enough for their youngest player to develop into a star.

Collins' defense-first team held a Celtics squad that included Paul Pierce, Ray Allen, Kevin Garnett, and Rajon Rondo to a mere 75 points. The Sixers won the game and forced a Game 7 against their long-time rivals.

A national sensation as a high school player, Jrue Holiday entered the NBA with only one year of college experience. As a freshman at UCLA, he had averaged nine points,

While the 76ers lost a hard-

four assists and four rebounds per game. The numbers weren't bad, but they did not reflect his explosive potential. In the 2009 NBA Draft, 16 teams passed on Holiday before the 76ers snatched him up. Sixers fans should be thankful that in his one year in college, Holiday played alongside future NBA guard Darren Collison. Collison had been at UCLA for three years. In 2008-09 he retained his position as the team's starting point guard, and Holiday never got the opportunity to showcase what he could do at the position. Had Holiday started at the point for the Bruins, there's no telling how high he might have gone in the draft.

The Young Get Younger

With an average age of 25, the 2012-13 76ers were one of the youngest teams in the NBA.

During the offseason in which Jrue Holiday transformed himself into a NBA All-Star who would average 18 points and eight assists per contest, 76ers management was hard at work as well. On August 10th, 2012, Andre Iguodala was part of a four-team trade that brought

76ers All-Star Jrue Holiday and Mavericks point guard Darren Collison shared the same backcourt in 2008-09.

No Minor Achievement

On November 2nd, 2005, Andrew Bynum became the youngest player to ever play in an NBA game. He was 18 years and six days old.

Los Angeles Lakers' All-Star center Andrew Bynum to Philly. It was an exciting time for Sixers fans. While grateful toward Iggy for leading them back to the playoffs, fans couldn't help but think of other big men who had brought NBA championships to Philadelphia.

Bynum began the 2012-13 season sidelined by knee trouble, but the 76ers still had high expectations. Yes, they lacked experience. The 2011-12 Sixers had been the league's youngest playoff team; the 2012-13 team was even younger. But Jrue Holiday, Thaddeus Young, Lavoy Allen, and the explosive Evan Turner had all played big minutes and made significant contributions during the 2012 playoff run. They knew what they were capable of when they followed their coach, believed in one another, and played smart, tough basketball. The only thing that remained to be seen was just how good they could be when the 25-year-old seven-footer that many called the best offensive center in the league was added to the mix.

Unfortunately for Sixers fans, the 2012-13 season was a disappointment. Holiday's inspired play was cause for celebration, but as the year progressed, the news regarding Bynum's knees just got worse. In March of 2013, Bynum underwent season-ending arthroscopic surgery on both knees.

He had not played a single game for his new team.

76ers management had hoped that Bynum might come to Philly and bring the kind of frontcourt scoring that they hadn't featured since the days of Moses and Wilt. For them, Bynum's injury was a bitter pill to swallow. But the evolution of Jrue Holiday into an All-Star and the continued growth of players like Thaddeus Young and Evan Turner, are sources of optimism for management and fans alike.

It's impossible to know what the future holds for the Philadelphia 76ers. But fans should take solace in the fact that while Eastern Conference teams have gotten older, the Sixers have gotten both younger and more experienced.

Evan Turner soars above the rim for a two-handed slam.

From Allen Iverson to Sir Charles to Moses to Dr. J to Wilt the Stilt, the great 76ers teams of the past have always had exceptional leaders. The question on the minds of today's Sixers fans is: Can Jrue Holiday lead this core of selfless, playoff-tested youngsters back to the peak of the sport? The city of Philadelphia waits for an answer.

WITHDRAWAL